The Chronological History of Cyprus

From Prehistoric Cyprus to Modern Cyprus and until 2018

Marios Adamides

2018

The Chronological History of Cyprus
From Prehistoric Cyprus to Modern Cyprus and until 2018

Prehistorical Cyprus

-Eteocypriots: The first inhabitants of Cyprus seem to have been farmers originated from Anatolia and the Levant. They spoke a pre-Indo-European language that the Greeks called "Eteocypriot" (meaning "true Cypriot") They ruled over the island during most of the bronze age known mostly as the kingdom of Alashiya, the prime exporter or copper in the entire region.

-Achaean (or Mycenaean) Greeks were living in Cyprus from the 14th century BC, yet most of them inhabited the island after the Trojan war. Achaeans were colonizing Cyprus from 1210 to 1000 BC. They established their cities which would later evolve into independent city-states in the "classical" Greek style. Thus began a process of "hellenization" of the island and influx of Greek inhabitants that lasted until Alexander's time when the Eteocypriot language was essentially extinct.

-Dorian Greeks arrived around 1100 BC and, unlike the pattern on the Greek mainland, the evidence suggests that they settled in Cyprus peacefully.

-Phoenicians: In the 8th century BC, several Phoenician colonies were founded, like Kart-Hadash (New Town), present day Larnaca and Salamis (Famagusta). Phoenicians were a thalassocratic ancient Semitic civilization that originated in the Eastern Mediterranean and in the west of the Fertile Crescent.

Scholars generally agree that it included the coastal areas of today's Lebanon, northern Israel and southern Syria.

The Prehistoric Period came to an end with the writing of the first works that still survive, first by the Assyrians, then by Greeks and Romans.

Ancient Cyprus

-**Assyrians:** The first written source shows Cyprus under Assyrian rule. A stela found in 1845 in Kition (Larnava) commemorates the victory of king Sargon II (721–705 BC) in 709 over the seven kings in Cyprus. The Assyrian Empire, was a major Semitic speaking Mesopotamian kingdom and empire of the ancient Near East and the Levant.

-**Egyptians**: Cyprus gained independence for some time around 669 BC but was conquered by **Egypt** under Amasis (570–525).

-**Persians:** The island was conquered by the **Persians** around 545 BC. A Persian palace has been excavated in the territory of Marion on the North coast near Soli. The inhabitants took part in the Ionian rising. At the beginning of the 4th century BC, Evagoras I, King of Salamis, took control of the whole island and tried to gain independence from Persia. Another uprising took place in 350 but was crushed by Artaxerxes in 344.

-During the siege of Tyre, the Cypriot Kings went over to **Alexander the Great.**

-**Ptolemeans**: In 321 four Cypriot kings sided with **Ptolemy I** and defended the island against Antigonos. Ptolemy lost Cyprus to

Demetrios Poliorketes in 306 and 294 BC, but after that it remained under Ptolemaic rule till 58 BC. It was ruled by a governor from Egypt and sometimes formed a minor Ptolemaic kingdom during the Hellenistic power-struggles of the 2nd and 1st centuries. Strong commercial relationships with Athens and Alexandria, two of the most important commercial centers of antiquity, developed.

Full Hellenisation only took place under Ptolemaic rule. Phoenician and native Cypriot traits disappeared, together with the old Cypriot syllabic script. A number of cities were founded during this time, e.g. Arsinoe that was founded between old and new Paphos by Ptolemy II.

-**Romans**: Cyprus became a Roman province in 58 BC, according to Strabo because the Roman politician, Publius Clodius Pulcher, held a grudge against the king of Cyprus, Ptolemy, and sent Marcus Cato to conquer the island after he had become tribune. Mark Antony gave the island to Cleopatra VII of Egypt and her sister Arsinoe IV, but it became a Roman province again after his defeat at the Battle of Actium in 30 BC. From 22 BC it was a senatorial province. The island suffered great losses during the Jewish rising of 115/116 AD.

After the reforms of Diocletian it was placed under the control of the Consularis Oriens and governed by a proconsul. Several earthquakes led to the destruction of Salamis at the beginning of the 4th century, at the same time drought and famine hit the island.

-The apostle Paul is reported to have **converted the people of Cyprus to Christianity**. The Levite Barnabas, a Cypriot, travelled to Cyprus and Anatolia with Paul (Acts. 12, 13). During the 5th century AD, the church of Cyprus achieved its independence from the Patriarch of Antioch at the Council of Ephesus in 431.

Cyprus in the Middle Ages

-Byzantines: After the division of the Roman Empire into an eastern half and a western half, Cyprus came under the rule of Byzantium. At that time, its bishop, while still subject to the Church in Constantinople, was made autocephalous by the Council of Ephesus.

-Arabs: In 649 AD the Arabs made the first attack on the island under the leadership of Muawiyah I. They conquered the capital Salamis - Constantia after a brief siege, but drafted a treaty with the local rulers. In the course of this expedition a relative of Muhammad, Umm-Haram, fell from her mule near the Salt Lake at Larnaca and was killed. She was buried at that spot and the Hala Sultan Tekke was built there in Ottoman times. Under Abu'l-Awar, the Arabs returned in 650 and installed a garrison of 12,000 on part of the island, where they remained until 680.

In 688, the emperor Justinian II and the caliph Abd al-Malik reached an unprecedented agreement. For the next 300 years, Cyprus was ruled jointly by both the Arabs and the Byzantines as a **condominium**, despite the nearly constant warfare between the two parties on the mainland. The Byzantines recovered control over the island for short periods thereafter, but the *status quo* was always restored.

This period lasted until the year 965 AD, when Niketas Chalkoutzes conquered the island for a resurgent Byzantium.

In 1185, the last Byzantine governor of Cyprus, **Isaac Comnenus** of Cyprus from a minor line of the Imperial house, rose in rebellion and attempted to seize the throne. His attempted coup was unsuccessful, but Comnenus was able to retain control of the island.

-**Richard the Lionheart:** In the 12th century AD the island became a target of the crusaders. Richard the Lionheart landed in Limassol on 1 June 1191 in search of his sister and his bride Berengaria, whose ship had become separated from the fleet in a storm. Richard's army landed when Isaac refused to return the hostages (Richard's sister, his bride, and several shipwrecked soldiers), and forced Isaac to flee from Limassol. He eventually surrendered, conceding control of the island to the King of England. Richard married Berengaria in Limassol on 12 May 1192. She was crowned as Queen of England by John Fitzluke, Bishop of Évreux. The crusader fleet continued to St. Jean d'Acre (Syria) on 5 June.

-**Knights Templar:** The army of Richard the Lionheart continued to occupy Cyprus and raised taxes. He sold the island to the Knights Templar in 1191 AD.

-**Lusignans:** In 1192 the French (House of Lusignans) occupied the island, establishing the Kingdom of Cyprus. They declared Latin the official language, later replacing it with French; much later, Greek was recognized as a second official language. In 1196, the Latin Church was established, and the Orthodox Cypriot Church experienced a series of religious persecutions. Maronites settled on Cyprus during the crusades and still maintain some villages in the North.

Amalric I of Cyprus received the royal crown and title from Henry VI, Holy Roman Emperor. A small minority Roman Catholic population of the island was mainly confined to some coastal cities, such as Famagusta, as well as inland Nicosia, the traditional capital.

Roman Catholics kept the reins of power and control, while the Greek inhabitants lived in the countryside; this was much the same as the arrangement in the Kingdom of Jerusalem.

The independent Eastern Orthodox Church of Cyprus, with its own archbishop and subject to no patriarch, was allowed to remain on the island, but the Latin Church largely displaced it in stature and holding property.

After the death of Amalric of Lusignan, the Kingdom continually passed to a series of young boys who grew up as king. The Ibelin family, which had held much power in Jerusalem prior to its downfall, acted as regents during these early years. In 1229 one of the Ibelin regents was forced out of power by Frederick II, Holy Roman Emperor, who brought the struggle between the Guelphs and Ghibellines to the island.

-**Mameluks:** The kingdom eventually came to be dominated more and more in the 14th century by the **Genoese merchants**. Cyprus therefore sided with the Avignon Papacy in the Western Schism, in the hope that the French would be able to drive out the Italians. The Egyptian Mameluks then made the kingdom a tributary state in 1426;

-**Venicians:** The remaining monarchs gradually lost almost all independence, until 1489 when the **last Queen, Catherine Cornaro**, was forced to sell the island to Venice.

Cyprus was under the Republic of Venice from 1489-1571 - <u>82 years.</u>

Modern History

-**Ottomans**: Cyprus under the Ottoman Empire from 1571-1878 - <u>307 years</u>.

Ottomans started raiding Cyprus since 1490, and captured it in 1571.

This is the historical setting to Shakespeare's *Othello*, the play's title character being the commander of the Venetian garrison defending Cyprus against the Ottomans.

-**British**:1878-1960 - <u>82 years</u>. In 1878, as the result of the Cyprus Convention, the United Kingdom took over the government of Cyprus as a protectorate from the Ottoman Empire. In 1914, at the beginning of World War I, Cyprus was annexed by the United Kingdom. In 1925, following the dissolution of the Ottoman Empire, Cyprus was made a **Crown Colony**.

1955 - Greek Cypriots begin guerrilla war against British rule. The guerrilla movement, the National Organisation of Cypriot Combatants (EOKA), wants enosis (unification) with Greece. British authorities arm a paramilitary police force made up of Turkish Cypriots.

1956 - Archbishop Makarios, head of enosis campaign, deported to the Seychelles after talks about self-government collapse on 29 February 1956.

1959 - Archbishop Makarios returns and is elected President of an independent Republic of Cyprus.

1960 - Independence of Cyprus

16 August - Cyprus gains independence after Greek and Turkish communities reach agreement on a bicommunal constitution. Treaty of Guarantee gives Britain, Greece and Turkey the right to intervene "to reestablish the state of affairs created by the present Treaty". Britain retains sovereignty over two military bases.

1963 - Makarios raises Turkish fears by proposing constitutional changes which would abrogate power-sharing arrangements. Inter-communal violence erupts in December 1963. Turkish side withdraws from power-sharing. Nicosia the capital is divided into Greek-Cypriot and Turkish-Cypriot sector with the setting up of the "green line".

1964 – Bloody ethnic confrontations between Greek-Cypriot and Turkish-Cypriot Communities with nearly 1000 casualties. United Nations peacekeeping force set up. Turkish Cypriots withdraw into 11 defended enclaves, 5% of the territory which included a sector in each of the five Cypriot towns.

1967 – Turkey threatens to invade Cyprus and Greek Military Division in Cyprus withdraws.

1974 – Turkish Invasion and Partition.

-Military junta in Greece organizes coup on 15 July 1974 against President Makarios, who escapes. Cyprus under Greek control and an appointed government is set up. Within 5 days, on 20 July 1974, Turkish troops land in the north.

-Coup collapses. Turkish forces occupy a third of the island, enforce partition between north and south occupying 37% of territory. About 165,000 Greek Cypriots flee or are driven from the Turkish-occupied north, and about 45,000 Turkish Cypriots leave the south for the north. The UN Security Council unanimously passes a resolution calling on Turkey to withdraw its troops from Cyprus. Turkey refuses to do so, despite repeated UN Security Council resolutions making the same demand over the following decades. Glafcos Clerides, president of the House of Representatives, becomes president until Makarios returns in December 1974.

1975 -Turkish Cypriots establish independent administration, with Rauf Denktash as president. Denktash and Clerides agree on population exchange crystallizing the ethnic division of Cyprus.

1977 - Makarios and Denktash reach a first High Level Agreement in February setting the goal of a **bi-communal federal republic** as a basis for negotiations.

-Makarios dies in 3 August 1977, after 27 years as President. He was succeeded by Spyros Kyprianou.

1979 – 2nd High Levi Agreement between Greek-Cypriots and Turkish-Cypriots.

1980 - UN-sponsored peace talks resume.

1983 - Denktash suspends talks and proclaims <u>Turkish Republic of Northern Cyprus (TRNC)</u>. It is recognised only by Turkey.

1985 - No agreement at talks between Denktash and Kyprianou.

1988 - Georgios Vassiliou elected Greek Cypriot president. 1989 - Vassiliou-Denktash talks abandoned.

1992 - Talks resume and collapse again.

1993 - Glafcos Clerides replaces Vassiliou as President at the age of 74 promising to bury the "Gali Ideas" of the UN Secretary General.

1994 - European Court of Justice rules that a list of goods, including fruit and vegetables, are not eligible for preferential treatment when exported by the Turkish Cypriot community directly to the EU.

1996 - Increased tension, violence along buffer zone in which two Greek Cypriot men were killed.

1997 - Failure of UN-mediated peace talks between Clerides and Denktash.

1998 - Clerides re-elected to a second term by narrow margin at the age of 79. EU lists Cyprus as potential member. Clerides' government threatens to install Russian-made anti-aircraft missiles S300. Turkey threatens military action. Clerides decides not to deploy the missiles.

2001

-June - UN Security Council renews its 36-year mission. Some 2,400 peacekeepers patrol the buffer zone (3.8% of the territory) between Greek and Turkish Cypriots.

-July - Dozens of police officers are injured as protesters attack a British military base at Akrotiri over plans to build telecommunications masts alleged to pose a health hazard.

-November - Turkey threatens to annex the north if the Republic of Cyprus joins the EU. It says the move coming before any reunification settlement, would violate the 1960 treaty.

2002

-January - Clerides and Denktash begin UN-sponsored negotiations. Minds are concentrated by EU membership aspirations.

-November - UN Secretary General Kofi Annan presents a comprehensive peace plan for Cyprus which envisages a federation with two constituent parts, the Greek-Cypriot State and the Turkish-Cypriot State.

-December - EU summit in Copenhagen invites Cyprus to join in 2004 provided the two communities agree to UN plan by early spring 2003. Without reunification, only the internationally recognised Greek Cypriot part of the island will gain membership.

2003

-February - Tassos Papadopoulos defeats Clerides in presidential elections.

-March - UN deadline for agreement on reunification plan passes. Secretary-General Kofi Annan acknowledges that the plan has failed.

-April - Turkish and Greek Cypriots cross island's dividing "green line" for first time in 29 years after Turkish Cypriot authorities ease border restrictions.

2004 European Union Membership

-April - Twin referendums on whether to accept UN reunification plan in last-minute bid to achieve united EU entry. Plan is endorsed by Turkish Cypriots but overwhelmingly rejected by Greek Cypriots. Turkish Cypriot leader Denktash stood down after decades in politics.

-1st May 2004 - Cyprus is one of 10 new states to join the EU, but does so as a divided island.

-December - Turkey agrees to extend its EU customs union agreement to 10 new member states, including Cyprus. The Turkish prime minister says this does not amount to a formal recognition of Cyprus.

2005

April - Mehmet Ali Talat elected as Turkish Cypriot president.

-May - Greek Cypriot and UN officials begin exploratory talks on prospects for new diplomatic peace effort.

-August - Cypriot airliner "Helios" crashes near Athens, Greece, killing all 121 passengers and crew. It is the island's worst peacetime disaster.

2006

-May - Greek Cypriots back ruling coalition in parliamentary elections, endorsing its opposition to reunification efforts.

-July - UN-sponsored talks between President Papadopoulos and Turkish Cypriot leader Mehmet Ali Talat. Agreement on a series of confidence-building measures and contacts between the two communities.

-November - EU-Turkey talks on Cyprus break down over Turkey's continued refusal to open its ports to traffic from the Republic of Cyprus. Turkey says the EU should end the isolation of the Turkish Cypriot community before Turkey opens its ports.

2007

-January-March - Greek and Turkish Cypriots demolish barriers dividing the old city of Nicosia. The moves are seen as paving the way for another official crossing point on what used to be a key commercial thoroughfare.

2008

January 1 - Cyprus adopts the euro.

-February - Left-wing leader Demetris Christofias wins presidential elections. He promises to work towards reunification.

-March - President Christofias and Turkish Cypriot leader Mehmet Ali Talat agree to start formal talks on reunification.

-April - Symbolic Ledra Street crossing between the Turkish and Greek sectors of Nicosia reopened for first time since 1964, i.e. after 44 years.

-September - Greek and Turkish Cypriot leaders launch intensive negotiations aimed at ending the division of the island.

2009

-April - Right-wing nationalist National Unity Party wins parliamentary elections in northern Cyprus, hampering peace talks. Turkish Cypriot leader Mehmet Ali Talat remains in office, but in a weakened position. Reunification talks continue through 2009, with little progress.

2010

-50 years of Cyprus's Independence.

-January - President Christofias and Turkish Cypriot leader Mehmet Ali Talat resume talks on reunification in downbeat mood, no progress made.

-April - Dervis Eroglu, who favours independence, wins the Turkish north's leadership contest, beating pro-unity incumbent Mehmet Ali Talat.

-May - Re-unification talks resume with a new hardliner representing the Turkish north.

2011

-May - Parliamentary polls. The main rightwing opposition party DISY wins by a narrow margin.

-July - Navy chief Andreas Ioannides and 12 others die when people when impounded Iranian containers of explosives blow up at the main naval base and the country's main power plant at Mari. The defence minister, military chief and foreign minister resign over the incident, which officials say occurred after a bush fire ignited the explosives.

-May - Fitch cut Cyprus's rating to A- from AA- in May over Greek debt fears. Cyprus could not sell state bonds in international markets.

-Credit rating agency Moody's cuts Cyprus's rating by two notches from A2 to BAA1, increasing risk of Cyprus requiring an EU bailout. Power shortages caused by the naval base blast knocking out the country's main power station, plus significant Greek debt, make financial reform difficult.

-August - President Christofias appoints a new cabinet with economist Kikis Kazamias from his AKEL party as finance minister. The previous cabinet resigned after the power shortages prompted the departure from the coalition government of the centre-right party DIKO.

-September - Cyprus begins exploratory drilling for oil and gas, prompting a diplomatic row with Turkey, which responds by sending an oil vessel to waters off northern Cyprus.

-October - President Christofias rejects the findings of an official report accusing him of "personal responsibility" for the July naval base blast on the grounds that he had been allegedly aware of the risk. Turkey's Turkish Petroleum Corporation begins drilling for oil and gas onshore in northern Cyprus despite protests from the Cypriot government that the action is illegal.

2012

-June - Cyprus appeals to European Union for financial assistance to shore up its banks, which are heavily exposed to the stumbling Greek economy.

-November - Cyprus says it has reached an "in-principle agreement" with the European Commission, the European Central Bank and the IMF on the terms of a bailout deal. The actual size of the bailout is to be determined following an investigation into the country's ailing banks.

2013 Deposits Haircut and Economic Memorandum

-February - Democratic Rally conservative candidate Nicos Anastasiades beats AKEL Communist party candidate Stavros Malas by a large margin in the presidential election run-off and succeeds Demetris Christofias as president. 2013

-March - President Anastasiades secures 10bn-euro bank bailout from the European Union and IMF with a 9 billion haircut of deposits from the two biggest Cyprus Banks. Laiki Bank, the country's second-biggest, is wound down and deposit-holders with more than 100,000 euros face big losses.

April - Finance Minister Michael Sarris resigns, citing an official investigation into the mishandling of the bailout. Until 2012 he was head of the collapsed Laiki Bank.

May - Cyprus receives 2bn euros - the first installment of a 10bn-euro bailout package - from international creditors. The European Court of Human Rights orders Turkey to pay 90m euros in damages to Greek Cypriots for the 1974 invasion. Turkey calls the ruling is unfair and says it will not pay.

2014

-October - Cyprus suspends peace talks with Turkish-held Cypriots in protest against what it calls efforts by Turkey to prevent it from exploring gas fields south of the island. The EU and US express concern over the tension.

2015

-January - The former Directors of the Bank of Cyprus are prosecuted in connection with Cyprus financial collapse.

-Mustafa Akinci wins Turkish Cypriot 'presidential' elections on a pro-reunification platform in April, leading to a resumption of Cyprus peace negotiations in May.

2016

-March - Cyprus exits its EU-IMF bailout programme.

-UN-facilitated negotiations to reunify Cyprus intensify and make good progress throughout the year. Anastasiades and Akinci fail to agree on <u>territorial adjustments</u> during November talks in **Mont Pelerin**, Switzerland. But both committed to continue negotiating.

2017

-**Crans Montana** Conference in Switzerland in June-July ends in a failure to agree on a solution of the Cyprus problem despite UN SG Gutierrez's "framework" for a solution.

-The Cyprus Economy grew by 4% in 2017, the third year in a row.

2018

-58 years of Cyprus's Independence.

- February - Nicos Anastasiades re-elected as President of Cyprus with 56%.

-March – Turkish warships prevent ENI, an Italian exploration company, to proceed in gas explorations in Plot 8 of Cyprus's EEZ.

April – A double homicide of a pair in Nicosia by a drug addict robber shocks Cyprus.

May – **Apoel of Nicosia** wins its 6th consecutive championship in Cyprus football.

THE ULTIMATE GUIDE ABOUT CYPRUS

1960-2018

(General Characteristics, Historical Background, Constitutional Framework, the Economy)

Marios Adamides
THE REPUBLIC OF CYPRUS

(General Characteristics, Historical Background, Constitutional Framework, the Economy)

1. GENERAL CHARACTERISTICS

Official Name: Republic of Cyprus (Dimocratia tis Kyprou or Kypriaki Dimokratia)

Flag: White with a copper-coloured outline of the island with two green olive-branches beneath.

Geographical Position: North-Eastern Mediterranean in the Middle East, 33 degrees east of Greenwich and 35 degrees north of Equator. 75 kms south of Turkey, 380 kms north of Egypt, 105 kms west of Syria and 380 kms east of the Greek island of Rhodes. There are two mountain ranges, one in the northern part (Pentadactylos) and the other on the southwest (Troodos), In between lays the Mesaoria plain.

Area: 9,251 Square Kms (3,571 sq miles)-Third largest island of the Mediterranean after Sicily and Sardinia. Maximum length of 241 kms from east to west and maximum width of 97 Kms from north to south.

Capital: Nicosia (Divided in Greek-Cypriot sector and Turkish-Cypriot sector) population 200,000) Other Towns: Limassol (Main Port), Larnaca (Airport), Famagusta (part of it abandoned since 1974), Kyrenia (Under Turkish occupation in the "Northern Republic of Northern Cyprus").   Ports: Limassol, Larnaca, Famagusta (North)   Airports: Larnaca, Pafos, Nicosia (closed since 1974), Tymbou (Ercan) (North)

Date of Independence: 16 August 1960 (Celebrated on 1st October)

Political Situation: Cyprus is divided since the 1974 Turkish invasion into two parts: The Republic of Cyprus recognized by all the international community except Turkey in the South (around 60%) where most Greek-Cypriots live, including around 200,000 refugees who were living in the North before 1974 and the so-called "Turkish Republic of Northern Cyprus" in the North (around 34% of the territory) recognized only by Turkey. There are around 130,000 Turkish-Cypriots, 120,000 Turkish nationals and 40,000 Turkish troops. 3% of the land is the so-called buffer zone separating the North and the South and guarded by the United Nations Force in Cyprus (UNFICYP) and 2.8% of the territory belongs to two sovereign British bases.

President of the Republic of Cyprus: Nicos Anastasiades(1.3.2013-1.3.2023)

President of the House of Parliament: President Demetrios Syllouris (2016- 5 year term)

Main Political Parties: AKEL (Left): General Secretary Antros Kyprianou), DISI (Center Right): President Averof Neophytou (2013)   DIKO (Center): President Nicholas Papadopoulos (2013), EDEK (Socialist): President Marinos Sizopoulos (2015).

Population: 880,000 (2016) in the government controlled area of which 180,000 (i.e 700,000 Greek-Cypriots) are foreigners and estimated 300,000 in the occupied area, including around 150,000 Turkish Nationals and in addition 40,000 Turkish troops.

Ethnic Composition: 83% Greeks (99.5% of the Greek-Cypriots live in the South), 15% Turks (98.7% live in the North), 2% others.

Religions: Greek-Orthodox (Greek Population), Sunni Muslim (Turkish Population), Catholic (Latins and Maronites).

Official Languages: Greek and Turkish (English is spoken widely).

Currency: Euro 1.1.2008

Government type: Based on 1960 Constitution. Presidential Republic. Greek-Cypriot President is both chief of state and head of government and is elected by universal suffrage for a 5-year term with no limitations as to reelection. Position of Vice-President reserved to the Turkish-Cypriot community is vacant since the 1963 communal strife. 10 ministers appointed by President who exercise executive power through the Council of Ministers.

Legal System: Codified Common Law (Cyprus was a British Colony from 1878-1960) with civil law (continental law) elements especially in administrative law and family law.

Legislative Branch: Multi-party, Unicameral House of Representatives, elected by universal suffrage, has 80 seats, 56 assigned to Greek-Cypriots and 24 to Turkish-Cypriots which are not filled.

International Membership: United Nations (1960), British Commonwealth (1961), Council of Europe (1961) European Union (1st May 2004), OSCE, OECD, WTO, WCO, IAEA. OPCW, the World Bank, the I.M.F etc.   Literacy Rate: 98%

Climate: Mediterranean with hot, dry summers from June to September and cool rather rainy and variable winters from November to March, separated by short autumn and spring seasons of rapid change.   Altitudes: Highest: 1.951 meters Mount Olympus, Nicosia: 180 meters

Time: +2 hours GMT, +1 hour compared with U.K, Germany, Italy.

International Code: CY   Internet Code: .cy

Television Stations: 2 public (CBC 1 and 2), 7 Private (Sigma, TVOne, Antena, TV Plus, Alpha, Capital, Extra).

International Telephone Code: 357-   22 (Nicosia), 23 (Famagusta), 24 (Larnaca), 25 (Limassol), 26 (Pafos), 99 (mobile phone numbers). Followed by 6-digit local numbers.

Daily Newspapers: 5 Greek newspapers and 1 English ("The Cyprus Mail")

Weights and Measures: The metric system.

Life Expectancy: Males: 76.1- Females: 81 (2001)

2. HISTORICAL BACKGROUND OF THE REPUBLIC OF CYPRUS

Cyprus gained its independence on 16 August 1960 from Great Britain which was the colonial power since 1878 (82 years of British Colonialism), succeeding the Ottoman Empire which controlled Cyprus since 1571 (307 years of Ottoman Occupation).The Constitution embodied the Zurich and London Agreements agreed between Greece, Turkey, the United Kingdom and the two communities on the island in 1959, the Greek-Cypriot and the Turkish-Cypriot.

At the same time with the signing of the Constitution on 16 August 1960 three other fundamental treaties were signed: the Treaty of Establishment of the Republic of Cyprus, the Treaty of Guarantee and the Treaty of Alliance, the former two treaties constituting an integral part of the Constitution as Appendix I and II respectively.

The deal of 1960 reflected the geopolitical interests of the United Kingdom and the USA, the balance of power between the guarantor powers and the preoccupation of Turkey that Cyprus should not become the last completely Greek island in the Mediterranean surrounding Turkey, following the annexation of the Dodecannesus to Greece from Italy after the 2nd World War.

The settlement upgraded the Turkish minority of 18% to a community of almost equal status with the Greek majority of 82%, aiming to safeguard the rights of the Turkish Cypriots and their share of power. Despite its deficiencies, the Constitution could function if the following factors had not been in play in 1960:

1. The Greek-Cypriots had waged a 4-year struggle (1955-59) against the British for "ENOSIS", i.e. Union with Greece. The 1960 arrangements failed to satisfy them but they accepted them fearing tri-partition (Macmillan Plan). If they were to accept an independent state, that state should recognize clearly the right of the Greek majority to govern without undue interference from the Turkish minority.

2. The first President of the Republic of Cyprus Archbishop Makarios (1960-1977) had little political experience in international relations, made miscalculations as to the real situation in Cyprus and the geopolitical interests involved and felt embarrassed when accused by his political opponents for having betrayed ENOSIS.

3. The Turkish side was adamant to enjoy all the rights and privileges vested to the Turkish Cypriot community under the Constitution and as a second option they would promote political and geographical partition if the circumstances allowed them to do so.

With these conditions in play it was not a big surprise that in 1963 a constitutional crisis took place after Makarios submitted proposals for 13 constitutional amendments. The Turkish reaction was immediately negative which in time led to the withdrawal of the Turkish Cypriot community from the organs of government and the creation of 12 Turkish Cypriot enclaves. The Green Line, separating the capital Nicosia in two parts, the Greek and the Turkish, was set up. Communal violence followed in late 1963 and in 1964 and Turkish planes bombarded Cypriot villages.

Turkey threatened to invade Cyprus but a strict diplomatic note from the President of the USA, Lyndon Johnson prevented the invasion, but resulted in creating Turkish discontent. A U.N peacekeeping force came to the island in 1964. Since 1963-4 the Cypriot Constitution is not strictly implemented and this has been achieved under the doctrine of necessity invoked by the Supreme Court of Cyprus.

In 1967 after a confrontation took place between the Greek-Cypriot army and Turkish-Cypriot militants in the villages of Kofinou and Ayios Theodoros, Turkey sent an ultimatum to Greece and Cyprus threatening to invade. The USA sent to the region as a mediator Cyrus Vance, who through shuttle diplomacy managed to diffuse the crisis, after Greece accepted to withdraw the Greek troops from Cyprus, sent secretly to the island after 1964,.

In 1974 Turkey invaded Cyprus after the Greek Junta staged a coup d' etat against President Makarios and established a controlled pro-union government in Cyprus. Since 1974 35% of the territory of Cyprus is under Turkish occupation (40,000 Turkish troops are stationed in Northern Cyprus) and the two communities, that were living all over Cyprus for centuries, live ever since separately in the two parts of Cyprus. Almost all the Turkish-Cypriots moved to the North and more than 180,000 Greek-Cypriots lost their houses and were evicted from the North.

In the Northern part of Cyprus the Turkish-Cypriots set up the "Turkish Republic of Northern Cyprus" in 1983, but this entity is not recognized by the international community except by Turkey (Security Council Resolution 541 (1983) condemned the declaration of the TRNC in 1983 and Security Council Resolution 550 (1984) called upon all states not to offer recognition and not assist in any way the secessionist entity). The only recognized government is the one of the Republic of Cyprus in the South, which is essentially a Greek-Cypriot state without the Turkish-Cypriot community sharing power and deprived of 35% of its territory, due to the 1974 events.

Since then a lot of efforts have been made to find a solution to the Cyprus problem with no avail. The last attempt was on April 24th 2004 when the Greek-Cypriot community rejected the Annan Plan which provided for the establishment of a bi-zonal, bi-communal federation. The Turkish-Cypriots voted in favour of the plan.

As mentioned before in 1983 the Turkish-Cypriots declared the establishment of the "Turkish Republic of Northern Cyprus" which is recognized only by Turkey, but since the referendum the international community aimed to enhance its economic, cultural and commercial relations with the Turkish-Cypriot community, without offering full state recognition.

Since May 1st 2004 the Republic of Cyprus is a member of the European Union and the accession includes all the territory although the European legal order (acquis communautaire) does not apply to the North until a solution is agreed upon by the two communities on the island. (Art. 1 of Protocol 10 of the Treaty of Accession of the Republic of Cyprus to the European Union).

The two communities of Cyprus agreed in February 2014 on a joint statement and started again negotiations to resolve the Cyprus problem based on a bi-zonal, bi-communal federation. The negotiations had reached a critical point in January 2017 with most issues agreed upon except the return of land to the Greek-Cypriot administration, the system of guarantees, the presence of Turkish troops and the concept of a rotational ethnic Presidency..

Some Cypriots have a lot to gain from a solution namely the return of their properties or compensation for them and a surge of economic development in the reconstruction of the divided city of Nicosia and the derelict part of the city of Amochostos in the East.

However, a strong current in the Greek Cypriot Community believes that a Bi-zonal Federation would mean that Turkey would have complete control of the new federated state an attitude that emanates from fear of Turkey, from Turkey's nationalist attitudes as well as the realization that it is almost impossible for a Bi-zonal Federation to function properly which is based on the strict separation of two communities with different ethnic background, religion and language and no tradition of political cooperation.

In addition the fact that the "Turkish Cypriot State" will be 40 miles from the Republic of Turkey signifies that it will be dependent and leaning towards the interests of Turkey rather than those of an independent "United Cyprus Republic". A Crimean style secession is a very strong possibility in case of future problems and antagonism with the "Greek Cypriot State". (Annan Plan terminology) in case of a solution based on a Bizonal, Bicommunal Federation.

If President Anastasiades and the Turkish-Cypriot Leader Akinci agree on a solution settlement this will have to approved by a majority of the people in two separate plebiscites. It is questionable that a Greek-Cypriot majority will accept the creation of a legal Turkish-Cypriot State in Cyprus politically equal to the Greek-Cypriot State in a Federal Cyprus.

In January 9-12 the two Communal leaders met in Geneva in Switzerland to find an agreement on all issues. On the 12th January they were joined by the three Guarantor Powers to discuss the security matters with no obvious results. The talks on security continued in 2017 at an experts level

On June 28 2017 a Conference on Cyprus was held in Crans Montana near Geneva .with the participation of the two Cyprus Communities and the three Guarantor Powers, the U.K, Greece and Tuyrkey. Despite the presence of the UN Secretary General the conference failed because Turkey insisted on the system of guarantees, right of intervention and the presence of Turkish troops for at least 15 years. The Republic of Cyprus and Greece would not accept such proposals that would have prevented Cyprus to become a "normal state". Opponents of President Anastasiades claimed that he was not prepared for a solution so close to the presidential Elections of February 2018. The Crans Montana failure can be considered as the end of the negotiating process which started in 2013.

After the Presidential Elections of February 2018, in which President Anastasiades was reelected, it is expected that a new imitative will recommence after a "period of reflection" of the two sides Nicos Anastasiades was the clear favourite to win the presidential elections, one reason being the division of the opposition and the other the clear weaknesses of the other candidates, Papadopoulos deemed immature, Malas an unknown geneticist by profession always ready to be a presidential candidate for the communist AKEL and Lillikas with no party support. If one adds to all this Anastasiades's political shrewdness, changing his narrative on the Cyprus Problem according to the audience and his broad political support based on clientelism, political appointments and favours it was not a surprise that he won re-election with 56%.

The exploration of the Exclusive Economic Zone will be included in the agenda of the Cyprus talks if a new process is agreed upon by the two parties. Turkey has made it crystal clear in March 2018 that she will not accept being excluded from gas explorations in the Eastern Mediterranean and the position of the government of Cyprus is that the Cypriot EEZ is not part of the Cyprus talks. It remains to be seen how these two opposing positions can be reconciled in a probable new UN initiative on the Cyprus problem.

3. CONSTITUTIONAL FRAMEWORK

The 1960 Constitution (199 Articles and 3 Annexes and 10 Amendments), which is still in force, recognized the existence of two communities on the island and established a unitary state based on partial communal autonomy. It set up a presidential system of government with a Greek Cypriot President and a Turkish Cypriot Vice-President with extensive veto powers, in the case of the Turkish-Cypriot Vice-President so as to safeguard the interests of the Turkish community.

Both the President and the Vice President had veto powers in matters related to foreign affairs, defense and security (Art.50). The Constitution provides for separate Communal Chambers and separate communal majorities in the House of Parliament in matters related to taxation, the municipalities and the modification of the electoral law (Art. 78). In addition Art. 173 provided for the setting up of separate municipalities in the five major towns.

The Treaty of Guarantee (Annex I of the Constitution) and the Treaty of Alliance (Annex II) formed an integral part of the Constitution (Art.181). Annex III contains the fundamental articles of the Constitution that cannot be amended by any means (Art. 182). Thus the Constitution of the Republic of Cyprus is totally inflexible. Since 1960 10 amendments of the Constitution took place that involved non-fundamental articles.

As has been mentioned before in 1963 a constitutional crisis occurred that resulted in the withdrawal of the Turkish-Cypriot community from the organs of government vested to them by the Supreme Law i.e. the Constitution (Art. 179). The Republic of Cyprus was in danger of collapse. The solution found by the Supreme Court was the legal doctrine of the law of necessity: the organs of government could function without strict adherence to the provisions of the Constitution as long as the circumstances warranted this drastic course.

Thus, since 1963 all the acts of the executive and the legislature are executed without the participation of the Turkish-Cypriot community. The checks and balances envisaged by the drafters of the Constitution do not exist anymore and a lot of provisions have become inoperative (The Supreme Constitutional Court, the Communal Chambers, the Institution of the Vice-President).

The result of the crisis of 1963 was that a bi-communal Constitution continued to function with the participation of only one of the two communities, the Greek-Cypriot, with the then President, Archbishop Makarios, as the dominant figure of the political life in Cyprus, since there was no Turkish-Cypriot Vice-President with whom to share the responsibility of ensuring the executive power (Art. 46).

The Annan Plan, rejected by the Greek-Cypriot community in the referendum of April 24th 2004 envisaged to transform the 1960 unitary state, based on partial communal autonomy, which functioned albeit with many problems from 1960-63 (since 1963 a political and geographical division of the two communities took place), into a bi-communal, bi-zonal federation.

The idea of a federation was accepted by the Greek-Cypriot community in 1977 after the 1974 Turkish invasion resulted in the partition of Cyprus in two geographical and ethnically-cleansed regions. The main bargain of the Annan Plan was the return of land and other property, lost in 1974, to the Greek-Cypriots in exchange of participation in the Federal Government of the Turkish-Cypriots, that they lost in 1963 when they abandoned all the positions assigned to them by the 1960 Constitution and the recognition of a Turkish Cypriot constituent state with extensive autonomy as one of the two components of the new Federal State, the so-called United Cyprus Republic.

4. THE ECONOMY OF CYPRUS

In 1960 Cyprus was a poor underdeveloped country with 45% of the workers involved in agriculture. Exports were mainly minerals and agricultural products. Hidden unemployment and underemployment were widespread and mass emigration was taking place.

In the 1960s and 1970s the Cypriot economy has been transformed into a rapidly growing economy with dynamic services, industrial and agricultural sectors and advanced infrastructures. The success can be attributed to a market-oriented economic system, sound macroeconomic policies, the existence of a dynamic and flexible entrepreneurial class, the small size of the population, the strategic position of the island and the inroads of money from immigrant Cypriots. The positive results of 13 years of rapid and sustained economic and social growth suffered a heavy blow by the Turkish invasion of 1974 and the occupation of 35% of the territory of the island. This area, the most productive and developed part of Cyprus in 1974, involved the Nicosia airport and the only deep water port of Famagusta.

By 1978 the economy recovered, grew ever since and full employment was achieved. In the beginning of the 21st century the economy was harmonized to meet the standards of the European Union and on May 1st 2004 Cyprus became a full member of the European Union joining a free economic market involving 25 European countries, 6 years after the beginning of accession negotiations in 1998.

Cyprus can be considered now as an open free market economy based on the provision of services and light manufacturing. The Greek-Cypriots enjoy a high level of life, the highest among their neighbors (Syria, Turkey, Lebanon, Egypt, Libya etc) and is a bridge between West (politically and culturally Cyprus can be considered to be essentially a Western country) and East (geographically Cyprus is in the Middle East).

The advantages of doing business in Cyprus include an educated English-speaking population, efficient communications, comparatively low costs, good airline connections, a sound banking system(until recently) and a unique position among three continents. The service sector, including tourism, shipping and trade, contribute 70% to the Gross National Product and employs 62% of the labour force. Industry and construction 24% and employ 25% of workers and agriculture accounts for 6% of GNP and employs 12% of the labour force. Potatoes and citrus fruits are the principal export crops. Cyprus has the 6th largest ship registry in the world and has a highly developed sector of international business companies (formerly called off-shore companies).

The main problems of the Cyprus economy were the vulnerability to external factors since it depended heavily on tourism, low productivity and high labour costs compared with competitive countries, a big deficit in the balance of trade and a rising fiscal and public debt, due mainly to the inflexible pay-roll of the civil servants accounting for more than 50% of the government expenditure.

Since 2008 the economic climate in Cyprus deteriorated seriously. The Cypriot government has been excluded from the international bond markets since May 2011. The "haircut" of the Greek public debt in 2011 was devastating for the two big Cypriot banks which needed huge financial support to survive. In the end a European Union bail out was agreed in March 2013 which included the winding-up of the second largest bank, Laiki Bank, and the haircut of 47% of the deposits of the biggest bank, Bank of Cyprus. The unemployment rate soared to 19% in 2014 and the banking sector has shrunk considerably. The Cyprus economic model set up after 1974 establishing Cyprus as a financial and banking sector collapsed and the public debt increased to 111% in 2015..

After three years in a Memorandum the Cyprus economy started to grow in 2015 after a drop of 11% of the GDP from 2011-2014. Cyprus came out of the European Union Memorandum with an expected GDP growth of 2.8 for 2016, yet with a public debt of

109% compared to the GDP (2016), the highest private debt in the E.U and an unemployment of around 12%. Also all major banks except one which has been saved by public money (COOP Bank) have been purchased by foreign funds. The increase of tourism arrivals by half a million reaching the record of 3,400,000 arrivals in 2017 was the major factor for the rise of the GDP by 2,8% in 2016 and 4% In 2017.

5. OTHER USEFUL INFORMATION

Important Web sites in Cyprus

1. Government of the Republic of Cyprus: http://www.Cyprus.gov.cy

2. Ministry of Foreign Affairs: http://www.mfa.gov.cy

3. Ministry of Finance: http://www.mof.gov.cy

4. Department of Statistics: http://www.mof.gov.cy/cystat

5. Public Information Office: http://www.pio.gov.cy

6. Phileleptheros, Daily Greek-Cypriot newspaper:

http://www.Phileleptheros.com

7. Politis, Daily Greek-Cypriot Newspaper: http://www.politis-news.com

8. Typos, Daily Cypriot on-line newspaper in English: http://www.typos.com.cy

9. Cyprus Mail, Daily English newspaper: http:///www.Cyprus- mail.com

Cyprus Officials

1. Attorney General: Costas Clerides

   (http://www.law.gov.cy)

2. Archbishop of Cyprus: Chrysostomos II

   (www.churchofcyprus.org.cy)

3. Governor of Central Bank: Chrystalla Giorgatzi

   (www.centralbank.gov.cy)

4. Auditor General: Odisseas Michaelides

   (http://www.audit.gov.cy)

5. President of the Supreme Court: Myron Nicalatos

   (http://www.supremecourt.gov.cy)

6. THE 7 PRESIDENTS OF THE REPEUBLIC OF CYPRUS

1960-2018

1st Archbishop Makarios III 1960-1977-<u>47 years</u> when he took over.

2nd Spyros Kyprianou 1977-1988-<u>45 years</u>

3rd George Vasiliou 1988-1993-<u>57 years</u>

4th Glafcos Clerides 1993-2003-<u>74 years</u>

5th Tassos Papadopoulos 2003-2008-<u>69 years</u>

6th Demetris Christofias 2008-2013-<u>62 years</u>

7th Nicos Anastasiades 2013-2023-<u>66 years</u>

Printed in Poland
by Amazon Fulfillment
Poland Sp. z o.o., Wrocław